D1709294

ENVIRONMENTAL DISASTERS

Bhopal
Chemical Plant Accident

by Nichol Bryan

WORLD ALMANAC® LIBRARY

Please visit our web site at: www.worldalmanaclibrary.com
For a free color catalog describing World Almanac® Library's list of high-quality books
and multimedia programs, call 1-800-848-2928 (USA) or 1-800-387-3178 (Canada).
World Almanac® Library's fax: (414) 332-3567.

Library of Congress Cataloging-in-Publication Data

Bryan, Nichol, 1958-
    Bhopal: chemical plant accident / by Nichol Bryan.
        p. cm. — (Environmental disasters)
    Summary: Presents an account of the 1984 chemical accident at the Union Carbide plant in Bhopal,
India, and its aftermath.
    Includes bibliographical references and index.
    ISBN 0–8368–5503–5 (lib. bdg.)
    ISBN 0–8368–5510–8 (softcover)
    1. Bhopal Union Carbide Plant Disaster, Bhopal, India, 1984—Juvenile literature.   2. Chemical plants—
India—Bhopal—Accidents—Juvenile literature.   3. Chemical plants—Accidents—Environmental aspects—
Juvenile literature.   4. Methyl isocyanate—Toxicology—India—Bhopal—Juvenile literature.   [1. Bhopal
Union Carbide Plant Disaster, Bhopal, India, 1984.   2. Chemical industry—Accidents.]   I. Title.
II. Environmental disasters (Milwaukee, Wis.)
    TP155.5.B78   2003
    363.17'91'09543—dc21   2003049718

First published in 2004 by
World Almanac® Library
330 West Olive Street, Suite 100
Milwaukee, WI 53212 USA

Produced by Lownik Communication Services
Cover design and page production: Heidi Bittner-Zastrow
Picture researcher: Jean Lownik
World Almanac® Library art direction: Tammy Gruenewald
World Almanac® Library series editor: Carol Ryback

Photo Credits: Cover, Pablo Bartholomew/Netphotograph.com; 4, 39, Heidi Bittner-Zastrow; 5, © Richard A.
Cooke/CORBIS; 6, 9, 21, 24, 25, 26, 27, 30(t), 33, 40, © Greenpeace/Raghu Rai; 7, 16, 28, © Bettmann/CORBIS;
8, Reuters/Kamal Kishore © Reuters NewMedia Inc./CORBIS; 11, © Chris Rainier/CORBIS; 12, © Joe
McDonald/CORBIS; 13, 37, © Greenpeace/Bane; 14, © Jeremy Horner/CORBIS; 15, Pesticide Action Network
North America (PANNA); 17, 42, Reuters/Raj Patidar © Reuters NewMedia Inc./CORBIS; 18, © Galen
Rowell/CORBIS; 19, 29, © AFP/CORBIS; 20, 23, 31, © Alain Nogues/CORBIS/SYGMA; 30(b), © Chandu
Mhatre © Bettmann/CORBIS; 32, AFP PHOTO ARKO DATTA © AFP/CORBIS; 34, © Greenpeace/Yashwant; 35,
AFP PHOTO/RAVEEDRAN © AFP/CORBIS; 36, © BALDEV/CORBIS/SYGMA; 41, © Greenpeace/David Adair

Printed in the United States of America

1 2 3 4 5 6 7 8 9 07 06 05 04 03

Cover: These two women are suffering from the effects of the gas leak
at Bhopal's Union Carbide plant. Their eyes are covered for protection
and to help speed the healing process.

Contents

.Bhopal
MADHYA PRADESH

INDIA

Introduction

Death
In the Night

Just after midnight on December 3, 1984, death came for more than two thousand people in Bhopal, India.

Some of the residents of this ancient city were asleep in their beds. Others jammed the local railroad station waiting for a late-night express train. Many more were crowded in public squares, singing and dancing at wedding celebrations.

Wherever they were, death took them, horribly. It came in the form

India is a country filled with contrasts. Ancient temples stand alongside modern buildings. Some people are extremely wealthy and others are extremely poor. While many parts of India are very technologically advanced, other areas lag behind the times. Farmers use pesticides and chemicals in combination with old-fashioned techniques — such as using oxen to plow fields.

of a cloud of toxic gas. Some died instantly. Others gasped their lives away, their lungs scared with chemical burns. Those who tried hardest to escape breathed in the gas most deeply and were often the first to die.

A runaway chemical reaction at the Union Carbide pesticide plant on the outskirts of Bhopal caused methyl isocyanate (MIC) gas to geyser from its tank. The blast was so powerful that the tank itself rocketed from its concrete container. Horrified plant workers looked on in amazement and

"So Many Have Died"
"We live right across the Union Carbide factory. So many people in our community are sick. So many have died. And people are still dying after they have been sick for a long time. People can't breathe properly, they often have fever, aches and pain in their stomach. Men and women have become weak."
— Kundan, a boy from Bhopal who was eight days old at the time of the disaster

Skulls and bones await disposal after research at the Hamidia Hospital in Bhopal. Medical experts believe the MIC affected the brain of many victims.

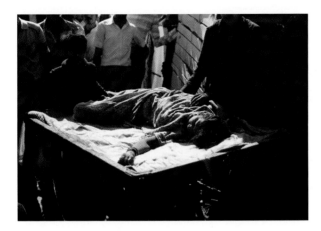

A few days after the incident, a boy pushes a cart holding a dead body. The leak killed thousands of people and blinded and burned thousands more. Dead cattle and other animals lay in the streets for days. Casualties were buried in mass graves or cremated in huge bonfires.

then ran for their lives. They knew something the other residents of Bhopal did not — that none of the safety equipment at the plant was working. Nothing could stop the spreading cloud of death.

About 46 tons (42 tonnes) of poisonous MIC spewed out of the tank for two hours. It spread out for nearly 30 square miles (77 square kilometers) over Bhopal, a city of almost one million people. As many as four thousand people eventually died from the effects of the spill. Ten times that many were seriously injured or even permanently disabled.

The toxic gas disaster at Bhopal would go down in history as the worst industrial accident ever. The world reacted in shock and horror to the news of the mishap. People wanted to know who to blame. Two decades later, people are still looking for the answer.

Many of the citizens of Bhopal, and the government of India itself, blamed the plant's U.S. owner, Union Carbide. They claimed that the giant corporation allowed the plant to fall into disrepair and ignored safety regulations. They also said the plant failed to warn the surrounding population about the dangers of a gas leak.

For its part, Union Carbide blamed the workers at the plant, all of whom were Indian citizens. The company claimed that workers did not follow proper maintenance procedures. At one point, Union Carbide claimed that the gas leak was sabotage by either an angry employee or a terrorist.

As time went on, the circle of blame grew wider. Frustrated, frightened victims said that the government of

In November 2000, victims of Bhopal protested for better compensation in New Delhi, India. They also demanded the trial of former Union Carbide chairman Warren Anderson.

"We Cannot Accept Responsibility"
"What we cannot and will not do . . . is accept responsibility for the Bhopal accident. It is therefore extremely likely we will face a number of protests at our sites around the world during the coming weeks, and into the future. I regret for this distraction — I realize it can be both disruptive and distressing — but I hope you can understand why we will not yield to this sort of pressure."

— Michael D. Parker, President and CEO of Dow Chemical Company, which bought Union Carbide in 2001

India and the state of Madhya Pradesh, where Bhopal is located, were acting too slowly to help them. Many victims said that the government wasn't seeking enough money from Union Carbide for their devastating injuries. Meanwhile, Union Carbide claimed that Indian authorities were interfering with its efforts to clean up the site and discover what caused the accident.

The legal and political battle spread to courts in India and the United States. In 1989, Union Carbide paid $470 million to India's government to settle a civil lawsuit. Victims still hope to bring criminal charges against Union Carbide and murder charges against former chairman Warren Anderson almost twenty years later.

The disaster also fueled a larger debate about many issues — the increased production of toxic chemicals in developing nations, the growing reliance on chemicals in agriculture, and the impact of huge multinational corporations on the countries where they do business.

"Some people in my neighborhood remind me that I stayed alive even though I was so small while so many people died. They make it sound like I brought on all this on the people. That makes me really sad."

— Kundan, a boy from Bhopal who was eight days old at the time of the disaster

Environmentalists warned that the death and devastation that happened at Bhopal could occur in other countries — even in the United States. Indeed, they say, it is happening right now, slowly, as chemical plants across the globe leak toxic chemicals into the air, soil, and water.

Environmental groups charge that corporations are shifting production of toxic materials from industrialized countries like the United States to

Gas Devi was born on the day the toxic gas swept across Bhopal. Her name means "gas goddess."

poorer nations, which often have lower emission standards and less stringent safety procedures. Chemical companies respond that they are providing jobs to people who desperately need them. In fact, despite the health and environmental risks, poorer countries often invite these types of corporations to build plants, believing that such factories will help the economy.

Everyone agrees that Bhopal was a terrible tragedy. But after all these years, there is little agreement on who was at fault, or even what really happened that night.

Government officials, industry leaders, scientists, and the general public remain divided on what action to take to prevent more "Bhopals" from happening.

In certain ways, we have not learned much from the tragedy of Bhopal, and we may never realize all of its lessons.

"Bhopal is the World"
"If we do not use history to educate people about the horrors of institutional inhumanity and violence, then we risk being silent accomplices in that inhumanity and violence. Bhopal is not only history. Bhopal is the world."
— Gary Cohen, Executive Director of the Environmental Health Fund, from his 1994 article, "Bhopal is More Than History," in *Green Left Weekly.*

11

 Chapter 1

A Beautiful
Plant

Bhopal was founded in the eleventh century by Raja Bhoj, the Pamar king of Dhar. He built a dam, or *pal*, that formed Bhopal's three lakes. In the 1700s, Bhopal became the center of the kingdom of Dost Mohammed Khan, an Afghan war chief.

Today, Bhopal is a bustling city in the center of Madja Pradesh — a large state in the center of India.

After India gained its independence from Britain in 1947, Bhopal began to grow. High-rise office buildings and housing developments sprang up

In 1969, Union Carbide built a plant in Bhopal, the capital of India's Madhya Pradesh state. After the plant was expanded in 1979, many workers referred to it as "the beautiful plant." By 1990, six years after the gas leak, the plant was no longer considered beautiful.

Famous throughout the world for its beauty, the Taj Mahal is located in Agra, India, about 336 miles (541 kilometers) north of Bhopal. (Agra was not affected by the Bhopal disaster.) Shah Jahan built the Taj Mahal in the 1600s as a mausoleum for his favorite wife, Mumtaz Mahal.

around its ancient markets, mosques, palaces, and surrounding forests and lakes. As the capital of Madja Pradesh, Bhopal attracted government offices, businesses and industry. By 1984, it was a thriving town of about 800,000 people. Most people from Bhopal are Muslims, but many Hindus and Sikhs live there, too.

Despite Bhopal's importance, many of its citizens remained very poor. More than 150,000 of them lived in makeshift huts. Water shortages and power cuts were common. The few telephones available seldom worked. In a way, Bhopal was a symbol of modern India, with wealth and technology living side by side with grinding poverty.

"Little Chance They'll Forgive You"

"It was really a beautiful plant. . . . It's true that you had a sense of danger when you went in there. But I had gotten used to living among toxic substances. After all, chemical engineers spend their lives in contact with dangerous products. You have to learn to respect them and, above all, you have to get to know them and learn how to handle them. If you make a mistake, there's very little chance they'll forgive you."

— Union Carbide engineer Warren Woomer, speaking of the Bhopal plant

Even so, the Bhopalese were particularly proud of the Union Carbide pesticide plant on the city's north side. The plant was built by Union Carbide India Limited to manufacture Sevin®, a chemical that Union Carbide promoted as a big boon for Indian agriculture and farmers.

Most people were excited about the plant and the promise of high-paying jobs. The company assured residents that the new facility would be "as safe as a chocolate factory." The Indian engineers who worked there called it the "beautiful plant."

Shacks built from scrap materials line an unpaved street in one of Bhopal's illegal shantytowns. Many casualties of the gas leak lived in Jaiprakash Nagar, a neighborhood just like this that sprang up directly across from the UCIL plant.

(Inset) A nine-year-old Nepali girl harvests tea on the Peshok Tea Estate near Darjeeling, West Bengal, India.

Large agricultural areas of India supply the world with produce. Field workers dry chili peppers in a field near Osian, Rajasthan, India.

Chemicals for a Green Revolution

India has undergone many severe famines over the course of its long history. In the early 1980s, its population — already nearing 800 million people — was growing faster than the food supply. India needed a dramatic solution. In the Green Revolution, it found one.

The Green Revolution completely changed India. By the end of the 1970s, it had gone from being one of the world's largest food importers to one of its largest food exporters. India became a model for other poor nations hoping to boost food production. And so its UCIL plant was not only important for Bhopal, but also for all of India.

India's Green Revolution relied on new types of wheat, rice, and corn crops. These varieties were hybrids — plants bred to produce some special characteristic. In this case, the plants were bred to produce more grain per plant. But the new plants needed more nutrition from the soil than the traditional crops. The hybrids were also more likely to be eaten by insects and attacked by disease.

Farmers used many fertilizers and pesticides to feed and protect their crops. As India's farmers grew more and more food on more and more land, their use

"There is No Danger"

"There is no cause for concern about the presence of the Union Carbide factory because the phosgene it produces is not a toxic gas . . . There is no danger to Bhopal, nor will there ever be."

— Madhya Pradesh labor minister T.S. Viyogi, answering a question on the Union Union Carbide plant's safety in 1982

of fertilizers and pesticides increased as well. By the 1980s, India was using pesticides on almost 200 million acres (80 million hectares). Yet, famine remained a huge problem.

But just as farmers in developing countries began praising the use of pesticides, these chemicals were coming under attack in the United States, where they had been used without restrictions or regard for negative effects for many decades.

Science helps build a new India

Oxen working the fields . . . the eternal river Ganges . . . jeweled elephants on parade. Today these symbols of ancient India exist side by side with a new sight—modern industry. India has developed bold new plans to build its economy and bring the promise of a bright future to its more than 400,000,000 people. ▶ But India needs the technical knowledge of the western world. For example, working with Indian engineers and technicians, Union Carbide recently made available its vast scientific resources to help build a major chemicals and plastics plant near Bombay. ▶ Throughout the free world, Union Carbide has been actively engaged in building plants for the manufacture of chemicals, plastics, carbons, gases, and metals. The people of Union Carbide welcome the opportunity to use their knowledge and skills in partnership with the citizens of so many great countries.

A HAND IN THINGS TO COME

UNION CARBIDE

WRITE for booklet B-5 "The Exciting Universe of Union Carbide," which tells how research in the fields of carbons, chemicals, gases, metals, plastics and nuclear energy keeps bringing new wonders into your life.
Union Carbide Corporation, 270 Park Avenue, New York 17, N. Y.

A 1962 Union Carbide advertisement promoting the benefits of chemicals, plastics, and "the technical knowledge of the western world" provides an eerie foreshadowing of the Bhopal disaster.

Rachel Carson (1907–1964) was an aquatic biologist who had worked for the U.S. Fish and Wildlife Service (USFWS). Her best-selling 1962 book, Silent Spring, influenced President Kennedy's Science Advisory Committee to order government testing of pesticides. Carson is credited with launching the "Age of Ecology."

In 1962, scientist Rachel Carson wrote about the commonly used pesticide dichlorodiphenyltrichloroethane (DDT). She warned that the chemical leached from farm fields and orchards into the food chain and drinking water. As people and animals consumed small amounts of DDT in their food and water, the chemical built up in their fatty tissues, causing disease and death. Carson titled her book *Silent Spring* after an imagined future in which most birds and animals had been killed by pesticides.

Carson's book became a best-seller in the United States and raised a lot of controversy about the use of chemicals in agriculture. By the early 1970s, the environmental movement was a strong political force in the United States.

President Richard M. Nixon responded to the issue by creating the Environmental Protection Agency (EPA), which was charged with keeping Americans safe from toxicants in their air, food, and water. Other laws limited the use of pesticides. One of the first to be banned entirely was DDT.

In the developing world, however, pesticide use continued to grow. Union Carbide, a corporation based in Danbury, Connecticut, was among the worldwide leaders in the production of pesticides. The U.S. company recognized India as a huge market for agricultural chemicals. It set up a partnership, called Union Carbide India Limited (UCIL), with Indian investors to produce pesticides and other chemicals at a plant in India.

UCIL selected Bhopal for its central location and its railway access. A ready workforce lived nearby, and the lakes surrounding the town would provide the water the factory needed.

The plant used MIC gas to produce carbaryl, a pesticide (a substance that kills pests, such as insects) with the brand name Sevin®. The plant also used MIC to produce a plant fungicide (a substance that kills fungi) with the brand name Temik®.

"Bhopal Will Be a Dead City"
"The day is not far off when Bhopal will be a dead city, when only scattered stones and debris will bear witness to its tragic end."

— From the article "Bhopal: We are Sitting on a Volcano," in the *Rapat Weekly* September 30, 1982

For ten years, UCIL imported the MIC it needed to make these pesticides. But in 1979, it began producing MIC right at the Bhopal plant. This change required a much larger facility, so the original plant was expanded.

Storing an atomic bomb

Union Carbide engineers knew the dangers of MIC. For storage, MIC must be pressurized to turn it into a liquid and stored at low temperatures. In its liquid form, MIC reacts with many common substances such as water and iron. These reactions produce enormous amounts of heat and cause MIC to expand from its container. Once released to air, MIC exists only as a gas. It is twice as heavy as air, and stays close to the ground, where its vapors irritate the eyes and lungs. MIC can also break down into a deadly gas called hydrogen cyanide, which causes almost instant death.

As dangerous as it was, MIC was not the only toxic gas used at the Bhopal plant. Other toxic gases included phosgene and monomethylamine. Yet Union Carbide assured city leaders in Bhopal that these chemicals would be used and stored with the strictest care.

Not everyone believed Union Carbide's assurances. In 1982, the local newspaper, *Rapat Weekly*, published a series of articles warning readers of the dangers of the chemicals being stored in their midst. The articles questioned the safety measures at the plant, and cautioned that it was only a matter of time before disaster struck. Still, many readers ignored the warnings.

Not long after UCIL enlarged the Bhopal plant, the company ran into financial difficulties. A series of severe

A man offers prayers on the eighteenth anniversary of the Bhopal disaster .

droughts in the early 1980s crippled India's farm economy. No one had money to buy the pesticides UCIL wanted to sell. Production of Sevin® at the Bhopal plant slowed to a trickle. With Sevin® sales down, the plant's managers were ordered to cut costs. UCIL reduced its staff and cut back on maintenance.

In 1982, Union Carbide sent a safety team from the U.S. to inspect the Bhopal plant. The inspectors found that equipment failures, improper operation, and lax maintenance created the risk of a toxic gas release. They recommended several changes to improve safety.

But UCIL's Indian managers never made the improvements. And nobody at Union Carbide headquarters in Danbury, Connecticut, checked that the changes were carried out in India.

Instead, in the fall of 1983, the UCIL plant manager ordered some additional cost-cutting measures. He shut down most of the plant's safety systems to save money. Several months before the accident, the refrigeration system that cooled the MIC tanks was shut off. A flame — called a flare — designed to burn off any escaping gases, was dismantled for repairs. A huge scrubber — which contained

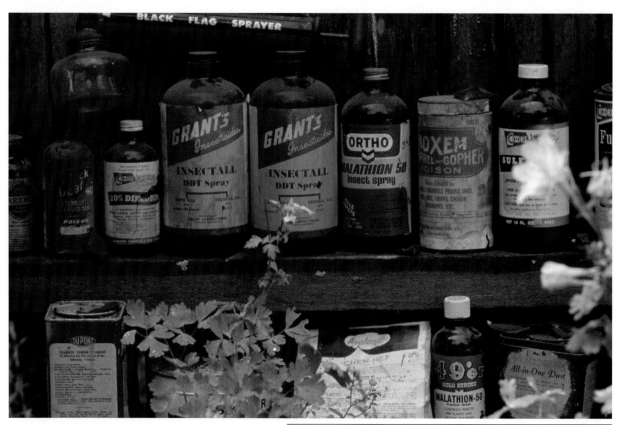

Until about the mid-1960s, a range of pesticides available in the United States and around the world contained DDT, a dangerous toxin.

A farmer examines his parched field near Chandigarh, India. A series of severe droughts in the 1980s caused crop failures and reduced the need for pesticides and other agri-chemicals. The lack of demand for pesticides shut down the UCIL plant in Bhopal.

chemicals that could help neutralize hazardous gases — was shut off as well. Finally, a last-chance system that could spray a water curtain around escaping gases proved too short: It reached to only 100 feet (30 meters); during the accident, the toxic gas spewed from a 120-foot (36-m) pipe.

Although the plant was not actively producing MIC, it stored more than sixty tons of it in tanks subjected to Bhopal's sweltering heat.

It is impossible to overstate the

danger presented by the improper storage of MIC. For instance, chemical engineers in France and Germany are hesitate to store MIC in amounts larger than 55-gallon drums (208-liter drums) because of its instability. In fact, chemists familiar with MIC prefer to make only as much as is needed at a time to avoid storing it at all. One chemical engineer who worked at UCIL in Bhopal but left before the tragedy, compared storing such large quantities of MIC to storing an atomic bomb.

Indian plant engineers, meanwhile, were confident that there was nothing to worry about — after all, the plant was shut down.

At Union Carbide's headquarters in Danbury, Connecticut, no one bothered to confirm that the tons of lethal gas were safely stored.

Bhopal officials took little interest in enforcing safety regulations. And the people were never told to cover their faces and breathe through a damp cloth in case of a gas leak.

All these factors came together to unleash a nightmare.

Many Bhopals

"There are numerous Bhopals scattered around the world, ongoing human and environmental tragedies caused by pesticide manufacturing facilities unchecked either by regulation or accountability to surrounding communities."
— Professor Angus Wright, California State University, Sacramento, 1991

Chapter 2

"The Worst Has Happened"

Things just weren't going right at the pesticide plant in late 1984. About a week or so before the accident, workers attempted to transfer some liquified MIC out of storage tank 610. In order to keep the tank pressure stable, they pumped nitrogen gas in as the MIC flowed out. But when operators tried to inject the nitrogen gas, it wouldn't go in because of a faulty valve.

A few days later, they tried the procedure again and encountered the same problem. No one bothered to fix the defective valve. And no one realized that the valve allowed water to seep into pipes around the tank.

That small amount of water reacted with MIC residue already in the pipes, forming a plastic buildup called trimer. The trimer that clogged the pipes could only be removed by flushing it with large amounts of water.

The evening of December 2, 1984, a workman at the plant, Rehman

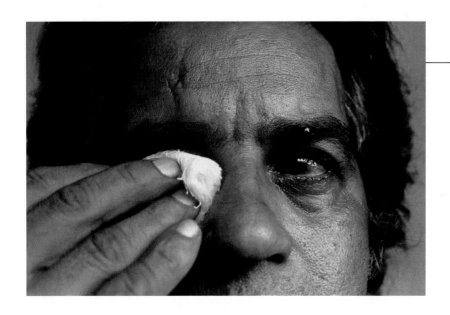

Toxic gases from the Union Carbide plant burned delicate eye and lung tissues. The gases also entered the bloodstream and damaged internal organs. Many survivors of the disaster experience lingering health and reproductive problems.

Khan, was ordered to perform the routine maintenance task of flushing out the pipes leading from the MIC tanks. Kahn had difficulty shutting off the main valve leading into the MIC tanks, but he did the best he could.

He then connected a water hose to begin the flushing. When Khan turned on the water, it backed up. So he turned it off and cleaned some filters. Everything seemed to work better after that. Khan left the water running, told his supervisor about his problems, and went off duty.

Around midnight, plant operators noticed their eyes were starting to burn. Worried about a leak, they checked the MIC tanks. An engineer spotted a small leak coming from tank number 610. He ran to report his discovery. The supervisor on duty, Shekil Qureshi, didn't believe it was possible for a non-operating plant to have an MIC leak. He told his staff members to calm down.

Despite Qureshi's assurances, workers at the plant felt uneasy. Pressure inside tank 610 climbed from 2 to 55 pounds per square inch (0.14 to 4 kilograms per square centimeter) in a short time. Worse, the workers could smell MIC, monomethylamine, and phosgene. Then a geyser of toxic gas shot from the tank. The men ran to sound an alarm. Qureshi finally realized that he had a disaster on his hands. He and his crew shut off all the valves

Shekil Qureshi was the UCIL plant supervisor on December 3, 1984. "The disaster unfolded before my eyes. My life has been wrecked and still I am being treated like an accused. I was badly exposed to the MIC."

to tank 610 to keep the reaction from spreading to other tanks. As they raced back to the control room, Qureshi turned and looked back at tank 610. He saw it burst out of its heavy concrete casing and stand straight up on end, propelled by a jet of poison gas. Even more gas shot out from a pipe that had broken when the tank ripped itself free.

"Nothing We Can Do"

"The worst has happened. There's nothing we can do."

— Union Carbide worker V. N. Singh, reporting the accident to his supervisor.

In desperation, plant operators attempted but failed to turn on the scrubber and the flare. Plant firemen tried to cool down the leaking tank with water without success. Two geysers of gas formed a cloud about 100 yards (92 meters) across.

Qureshi looked at a windsock flying above the plant and saw that the wind was blowing south — straight toward Bhopal. At that point, he knew there was no way to stop a catastrophe. He ordered his men to save their own lives.

A night of celebration

For many of the citizens of Bhopal, that night was one for celebration. Two important weddings occurred that day, with hundreds of family members and friends gathering in public parks to dance, sing, and enjoy fireworks displays. At the local train station, things were equally busy. Travelers crowded the platform. Many had chained their luggage to their legs to protect it from the thieves who hung around the station.

Asleep or awake, the Bhopalese had no way of knowing what had just happened at the pesticide plant. Some heard the alarm, but it stopped after a very brief sounding. False alarms around the plant were commonplace; most people ignored the siren. Soon, however, many of those at the outdoor parties noticed their eyes beginning to sting. Many recalled that the smell resembled burning chili peppers. Then

"Terror had Filled Me"

"It felt like someone was burning chilies. I got really scared and out of fear I opened the door. Outside everyone was running, screaming, nothing could be seen — the thick fog hung everywhere. It was clear that we were being poisoned. The stench of rotting potatoes was strong . . . Everywhere there were people running, vomiting, men and women wearing almost nothing . . . Terror had filled me from within. Street lamps looked as if they were dim candles burning. People's screams and shouts [were] dulled by the thickness of the gas fog."

— Jewan Shinde, a Bhopal resident

people began to cough and gasp as the MIC burned into their lungs. Horses and cows started to go mad from the fire in their eyes and chests.

In minutes, Bhopal became a scene from hell. Hundreds of terrified people were running in all directions, clutching children or possessions. Many simply fell down dead the instant the gas reached them. Others stumbled blindly in the thickening gas, struggling to breathe, finally collapsing in pain and exhaustion. Awakened by the screams and shouts in the streets, people already asleep sprang from their beds and joined the panicking masses. Many, realizing they could not outrun the poison cloud, tried to escape any way they could — on bicycles, in cars, or by jumping onto the backs of trucks. Any moving vehicle was mobbed by people looking for a fast way out.

The gas cloud hit the train station at about 1:00 A.M. Station operators looked on in alarm as people scrambled to get off the crowded platform. Those who had chained their luggage to themselves were hopelessly trapped. Soon a pile of bodies covered the platform. The dying lay gasping next to those already dead.

Station workers ran down the tracks to warn an approaching train not to stop. But the engineer missed their frantic signals and let his passengers off anyway. They quickly joined the ranks of the victims.

At the Bhopal police station, officers struggled to understand what was happening. Around 1:15 A.M., they received a panicked call regarding a large gas leak on the city's north side.

The police called Union Carbide's works manager, who told them he hadn't heard of any leak. Besides, he answered, there's no way the leak was from the Union Carbide plant: It was shut down.

The phone kept ringing at the station, with terrified citizens begging for information about what to do. The police, who had no idea what they were dealing with, advised people to stay indoors and keep calm. They kept calling the Union Carbide works manager, but were repeatedly told there was no leak.

At 2:15 A.M., Union Carbide's public siren went off again. Then a Union Carbide engineer appeared at the police station to report that the leak was plugged. It was the first confirmation of the disaster — more than two hours after the gas leak.

Bhophalese jam onto an outbound train eleven days after a cloud of MIC from the UCIL plant killed and injured thousands. The panic was prompted by the announcement that the plant would reopen.

The morning after the leak, survivors of the disaster gather in front of the Union Carbide factory. Their eyes and lungs were badly damaged by exposure to the gas.

Effects of the gas

By early morning, Bhopal's three hospitals began to fill up with victims begging for assistance. Doctors were stunned by what they were seeing. People were coming in and then dying by the scores, literally drowning as their damaged lungs filled up with fluid. Many had been completely blinded by the gas.

Doctors called Union Carbide to find out what chemicals these people had been exposed to. At first they were told nothing. Then the Union Carbide works manager admitted that MIC had been released, but that it was nothing but a "mild irritant." Meanwhile, doctors and nurses focused on comforting the thousands of victims while trying to deal with the hundreds of dead bodies that were piling up.

The MIC affected victims in many ways. Some of it broke down into hydrocyanic acid, which causes brain, kidney, and liver damage and almost immediate death.

Many more victims were affected by the MIC gas, which stayed close to the ground. The primary problem people experienced was burning in their nose, throat, and lungs. The burns in their lungs were causing the sensitive tissues to secrete fluids that quickly built up. This fluid buildup is called chemical pneumonia.

As the victims' lungs filled up with fluid, they had to struggle harder for breath. And as they did, they drew in more of the toxicants that were destroying their lungs. Those who fought the hardest to survive often died the fastest, because they breathed in and out very heavily.

In addition to their lungs, the MIC also attacked people's eyes. Many of the victims had severe burns to their corneas, the part of the eye that covers and protects the lens. At first, the burns looked so bad that doctors feared that 100,000 people would be permanently blinded. Fortunately, most eventually recovered their sight.

By morning, Bhopal was a city of death. In the shantytowns crowded around the pesticide plant, the huts were filled with the bodies of people killed in their sleep. Throughout the town, the streets were littered with corpses, tumbled next to the strewn belongings they had tried to save. Dead livestock, pets, and people lay everywhere. Bodies also lay scattered in the field and forests around the town where fleeing people had finally lost the struggle to survive.

For the dead, the nightmare of Bhopal had ended. For the living, the horror had just begun.

Long-Term Effects
Before the Bhopal disaster, not much was known about the long-term effects of MIC on humans. Doctors studying the Bhopal survivors have found that breathing the gas can cause lung diseases such as bronchitis and emphysema, as well as vision problems like cataracts. Several nervous system disorders have also been traced to the gas. They include loss of memory and motor skills. Anxiety and depression also appear to be related disorders.

Rubeda Banu's three sons have stunted growth. Shakeel (who was a week old when the tragedy occurred), Raes Ahmed (who was 18 months old), and Muzaffar (who was born a year later), are all less than five feet tall.

Chapter 3

Chaos and
Panic

In the days following the Bhopal disaster it became clear that neither Union Carbide, the Indian state and national governments, nor local medical staff had prepared in any way for such a widespread disaster.

The Indian prime minister, Rajiv Gandhi, called the event a historic tragedy and called on the world for help. State officials in Madhya Pradesh appealed to citizens to remain calm.

About seventy thousand people flooded into the local hospitals. When doctors had filled all the available beds and floor space inside, they started moving patients outside. Soon the roads around the city's main hospital were covered with makeshift cots filled with the wounded. From around the world, doctors rushed to India to help.

Just as urgent was the problem

Mass cremations were held alongside the communal graves in the days following the leak. "The bodies were strewn all over and the stench of death was overpowering," social worker Amar Chand Ajmera, 76, recalled in 1984. "I remember we cremated more than 2,000 bodies in a day."

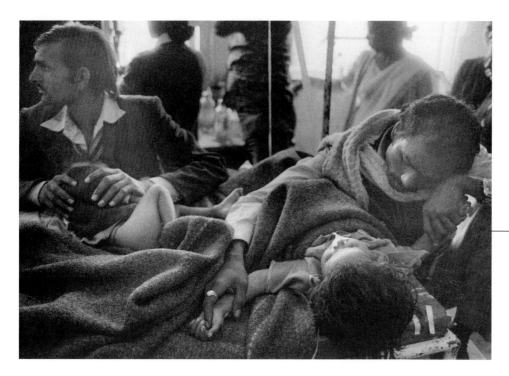

In the immediate aftermath of the disaster, thousands of sick children came to Hamidia Hospital. Their parents were too ill to care for them.

of what to do with the dead. Corpses had to be cleared from public areas or they would create a new health hazard. In all the chaos, it was hard to identify all the bodies, particularly

"Arrogance and Contempt"

"The scale and intensity of the Bhopal disaster boggles the mind. It is not only the thousands of people who have already died but the tens of thousands who, while they have survived thus far, are experiencing great physical suffering and emotional anguish. Virtually all are very poor and vulnerable. It is also the arrogance and contempt with which these powerless victims have been and are being treated."

— From a 1986 report for the Citizen's Commission on Bhopal

because entire families had been wiped out in so many instances. Religious concerns also made it difficult. According to their beliefs, Muslims needed to be buried immediately, while Hindu families wanted their dead cremated, or burned. Many bodies of Muslims were snatched up by grieving relatives just as they were being placed on a Hindu funeral pyre.

News of the accident reached Union Carbide headquarters. Company Chairman Warren M. Anderson announced that he would bring a technical team to India to help the government cope with the disaster and to investigate what had gone wrong. But before the search for clues could begin, plant operators had a more urgent problem to cope with: twenty thousand leftover tons of liquid

Warren Anderson, the chairperson of Union Carbide at the time of the accident, was arrested when he went to India shortly after the gas leak from the Bhopal pesticide plant. He is shown here speaking to reporters upon his return to the United States.

MIC remaining in tanks at the Bhopal plant.

The Indian Government launched Operation Faith, an urgent effort to avert a further leak at UCIL. Working with plant staff and a Union Carbide technical team, government agents ordered the remaining MIC to be removed from the tanks and processed into pesticides, which would be safer to ship out of the area.

When Anderson arrived in India with his technical team two days after the accident, he was in for a shock. An Indian court had charged him with "culpable homicide through negligence." In effect, Anderson had been personally charged with murder. So were J. Mukund, the plant's

"Possibly Eight or Twelve Fatalities"

"I had received my first notice of the incident through a telephone call from a colleague at 2:30 A.M. on Dec. 3. I was advised that there had been an 'accident' at a plant in India, that no plant employees had been injured, but that there were fatalities, possibly eight or twelve, in the nearby community. A meeting had been called for 6 A.M. in Danbury. On my way, I listened to news reports on my car radio as the death estimate rose to about 50. Later in the day, the number grew much larger."

— Jackson B. Browning, former Vice President of Health, Safety, and Environmental Programs for Union Carbide

manager, and six other Union Carbide employees. Anderson was arrested the moment he got to Bhopal. He was held for six hours and then released on $2,500 bond. He was driven to the airport in Delhi and urged to leave the country.

Union Carbide faced other obstacles when it tried to find out what had happened at the plant. The Indian Central Bureau of Investigation (CBI) had taken control of the facility. It would not allow documents to be removed from the plant. The CBI

"[Union Carbide] could not tell us exactly what is the toxic effect of the gas, and how best it could be treated. Secondly, they also did not tell us whether the information on this subject was available anywhere else if it was not with them. Thirdly, they did not give us any substantial help in carrying out treatment of these patients. Until four or five days later when a team arrived from their United States office."

— Dr. N. P. Misra,
dean of the Gandhi Medical College
at Bhopal

would not let local Union Carbide employees talk to the U.S. investigation team or to the press. Publicly, the Indian government said that they feared Union Carbide officials would tamper with evidence or try to influence witnesses. For its part, Union Carbide officials thought the CBI was trying to build a case that would make the corporation financially responsible for the disaster.

Global reaction

The survivors of Bhopal were numb with shock and grief. But they were also very angry. Within days of the disaster, crowds of protesters began to show up at the Union Carbide offices and the state government building. They were demanding that Union Carbide officials be brought to justice. They were also demanding better medical treatment and more information about the effects of the gases they had been exposed to.

Around the world, people reacted with horror to the Bhopal accident. Scenes of bodies littering the streets provoked anger and fear. People wanted to know how the accident occurred — and whether they risked a similar fate. Communities with chemical plants of their own began asking about the likelihood of toxic leaks of their own. Often, the answers scared them.

This blind woman is a victim of the gas leak. In 1991, she attended a rally commemorating the disaster. Her sign features former Union Carbide chairman Warren Anderson.

Dr. Sathpathy, the forensic expert at Hamidia Hospital, has been called the Death Doctor. "I must have performed more than 20,000 autopsies so far," he said in 2002. No relative of a gas victim can get compensation for a death without my certificate. It has been a nightmarish experience."

In the United States, there were hundreds of facilities that stored deadly chemicals on site. While there had never been a disaster like the one at Bhopal, there had been many smaller accidental releases over the years. Community officials realized that they often had no idea what toxicants were being used at local industries. Most had no plan for responding to large accidental releases. Local hospitals often did not have the equipment or expertise they would need in case of an accident. Frightened, many Americans began demanding changes from national and local governments.

Counting the losses

As Bhopal struggled to recover, one question that came up repeatedly was how many people had actually been killed and injured in the disaster. The number was not a mere statistic; the

No Place to Keep the Bodies

"There was such a terrible crowd that there wasn't even place to keep the bodies on the floor. As soon as a patient was declared dead, his relatives would vanish with the body. I saw at lease 50 babies taken away like this. I would estimate that anything between 500 and 1,000 bodies were taken away before their deaths could be registered."

— A doctor from Bhopal's Hamidia Hospital

Bodies lying outside Hamidia Hospital await cremation after identification by relatives.

Bhopal's shantytown residents were most affected by the poisonous cloud. The UCIL plant appears in the background.

Indian government had promised to compensate families for their dead and to provide assistance for the injured. The fatality and casualty toll would also be considered by judges and juries in determining the damages responsible parties would have to pay.

But estimates of the human toll at Bhopal varied widely. Documentation was poor. The mass burials and cremations that took place in the days after the disaster meant that much evidence had been destroyed. Many of the people who lived in the crowded shantytowns around the plant were jobless and homeless; there were no records to verify their existence after they died. Health conditions in the Bhopal slums had always been very poor, so it wasn't always clear when a death or illness was the result of the gas exposure or another cause.

The Indian government officially announced that 2,000 people had died in the disaster. By 1987, that figure had risen to 3,500. In 1992, the government revised its estimate again, saying that more than 4,000 had been killed. In addition, an estimated 30,000 to 40,000 people had also been seriously injured. Another 200,000 citizens were affected in lesser ways — they were slightly injured or suffered economic hardship because of the accident.

All those who had suffered — and were still suffering — from the effects of the gas were begging for help. They demanded justice. But help was slow to arrive.

Justice would take even longer.

Chapter 4

Grief Turns To Rage

Facing public outcry and charges of negligence, Union Carbide took steps to help the victims of Bhopal.

Days after the disaster, the company offered $2 million in assistance to the prime minister's relief fund. It paid to send doctors and medical equipment to Bhopal. In 1985, the company provided another $5 million aid and established a $2.2 million job training center in Bhopal.

But for the people of Bhopal, it was not enough. In 1985, the government of India passed the Bhopal Gas Leak Disaster Act, which gave it sole power to seek a settlement on behalf of the victims. By that time, 145 lawsuits had been filed against Union Carbide by some 200,000 plaintiffs. Most of these suits had been filed in the United States. But the U.S. judge in the case ruled that the trial of Union Carbide would have to be held in India.

A boy holds a sign showing a young victim of the Union Carbide gas disaster. The grim image on the sign has become a symbol of the tragedy.

The Indian government charged that Union Carbide intentionally cut back on safety features in the design of the Bhopal plant. It said the company had not ensured that the plant was properly maintained and operated. Union Carbide failed to follow up on its own 1982 safety audit. Union Carbide's neglect led to a situation in which contaminated water backed up into MIC tank 610 and caused a runaway reaction.

Union Carbide, on the other hand, said it was not primarily responsible for the Bhopal plant. It claimed its Indian subsidiary was responsible for plant maintenance and operation. What's more, it said the Indian government was responsible for inspecting and regulating the plant. If conditions at the plant created a risk of toxic release, it was no fault of Union Carbide headquarters.

But the lawyers defending Union Carbide went even further. They claimed that their investigation had shown that the gas release wasn't an accident at all. Instead, they said it was the result of a worker purposefully putting water into the MIC tank. They charged plant workers with trying to cover up the sabotage.

The trial of Union Carbide dragged on for more than seven years. In the end, Union Carbide agreed to pay the Indian government $470 million in compensation. The agreement would end all financial and criminal cases

"I remember making three tiered graves. There was no option but to pile up one body on top of another," says Mohammad Aziz. Soil and water movements since 1984 have pushed some skeletons out of the shallow graves.

against Union Carbide and its officers. Union Carbide also agreed to sell its interest in Union Carbide India, Ltd., and donate the funds to build a hospital in Bhopal.

Union Carbide officials called the settlement "more than generous," but victims groups were outraged. Many of the victims had been calling for billions of dollars in compensation from Union Carbide. The victims also wanted to see Union Carbide executives charged with criminal penalties. In 1991, they petitioned the Supreme Court of India to throw out the settlement. The court upheld the cash settlement, but said that criminal cases could go forward.

The continuation of the criminal trial meant that Union Carbide chairman Warren Anderson was still wanted for murder. Anderson never returned to India to face the Bhopal District Court, where the case against

By 1999, Union Carbide's Bhopal facility was neglected and rusting.

him was pending. In August 2002, almost eighteen years after the disaster, the Indian government tried to get the charges against Anderson reduced from culpable homicide to negligence. But the judge refused to drop the homicide charges. Instead, it ordered the CBI to start legal proceedings to extradite Anderson from the U.S. to India for trial. But he could not be found. Some said that Anderson had gone into hiding in order to avoid being removed from the U.S., but his lawyer denied it.

Union Carbide, along with the rest of the chemical industry worldwide, realized it needed to take steps to rebuild its image after the calamity at Bhopal. Chemical manufacturers were facing tougher regulations and more resistance from local communities

Union Carbide Claims Sabotage

"We believe . . . that a disgruntled operator entered the storage area and hooked up one of the readily available rubber water hoses to Tank 610, with the intention of contaminating and spoiling the tank's contents. It was well known among the plant's operators that water and MIC should not be mixed. He unscrewed the local pressure indicator, which can be easily accomplished by hand, and connected the hose to the tank. The entire operation could be completed within five minutes. Minor incidents of process sabotage by employees had occurred previously at the Bhopal plant, and, indeed, occur from time to time in industrial plants all over the world."

— From a 1988 report sponsored by Union Carbide

In 2002, protesters compared former Union Carbide chairman Warren Anderson to terrorist Osama bin Laden. The demonstration also targeted Indian Prime Minister Atal Behari Vajpayee's and Home Minister Lal Krishna Advani's alleged support of Warren Anderson.

where they wanted to build new facilities. In response to Bhopal, the Chemical Manufacturers Association developed Responsible Care guidelines in 1985. The guidelines set out standards for performance, communication, and accountability for chemical facilities. Under the voluntary rules, companies are supposed to inform local communities about what chemicals are stored on site and work to develop disaster plans. Responsible Care guidelines have since been adopted by manufacturers associations in forty-nine countries.

The U. S. Congress responded to Bhopal with a host of new laws. In 1986, it passed the Emergency Planning and Community Right-to-Know Act (EPCRA). This law requires states and communities to develop accident plans in case of toxic releases. EPCRA also gives individuals and communities the right to get information on which hazardous materials are being stored in their immediate vicinity.

For many Bhopalese, the payments and settlements made by Union Carbide simply cannot compensate for their loss and suffering. Ongoing protests remind Union Carbide, the Indian government, and the world of the horror unleashed upon them in December 1984.

In 1990, the U.S. Congress reviewed an alarming report by the Environmental Protection Agency. It listed seventeen U.S. chemical releases in the early 1980s that could actually have been more severe than Bhopal, if the weather conditions had been right or if the plants had been located closer to residential areas. The legislators decided to do more to prevent accidents in the future. They passed laws giving the EPA and the Occupational Safety and Health Administration (OSHA) a bigger role in preventing accidents at chemical facilities.

That same year, Congress created the U.S. Chemical Safety and Hazard Investigation Board, which was charged with investigating and reporting on the causes and probable causes of chemical

"Bhopal Is Continuing to Happen"

"Bhopal did not just happen on December 3rd, 1984, it is continuing to happen to those who were unfortunate to live in its vicinity on that fateful day. Not only this generation but the next generations too stands to be contaminated and poisoned by the disaster. Not only is the soil, but also groundwater, vegetables [and] mother's breast milk has [been] found to be contaminated."

— From a 2002 Fact-Finding Mission on Bhopal by Shristi, an environmental group that monitors trade in hazardous materials

incidents. The Safety and Hazard Board also conducts research on chemical safety in the hope of preventing major toxic releases.

Although chemical safety has improved in the United States, many environmentalists say that poorer countries are still at risk. These countries are eager to set up and maintain new plants, which provide jobs for citizens and tax money for the government. Industrial plants can also provide goods, such as plastics and

A Bhopalese woman (background, left) pumps nonpotable water — water that is unfit to drink — from a well near the UCIL plant for use by her family. Chemicals leaking from the plant continue to haunt residents decades later.

pesticides, which the country might import otherwise.

Critics say that developing countries often don't have the trained workforce needed to properly maintain these plants or the experts needed to regulate them. In case of an accident, poor countries don't have enough communications facilities, hospitals, and hazardous-materials teams to respond fast enough. What's more, they say, these countries become so dependent on the plants that they are afraid to crack down on health and safety violations.

The results, environmentalists say, are hundreds of "slow-motion Bhopals" spread all over the world. Not only do these poorly maintained plants present a risk of large toxic releases like the one at Bhopal, they often are releasing small amounts of poison on a regular basis. The air and water around them become contaminated, endangering the lives of the unsuspecting residents who live around them.

Activists picket for tougher restrictions on multinational corporations building chemical plants in the developing world. But right now, there is no international organization that can enforce such rules.

Does the poisoning continue?

While the tragedy at Bhopal is a fading memory for many in the world, it remains a focus of misery and anger for the people there. Doctors say that tens of thousands of people there still suffer many diseases, such as asthma and pneumonia, which were caused or made worse by their exposure to the gas cloud. They also say that the disaster is now claiming a second generation of victims. Stillbirths

"Case Closed"

The debate over who is responsible for Bhopal got even more complicated in 2001. That's when Union Carbide merged with The Dow Chemical Company. The merger made Dow the world's largest chemical producer.

Dow maintains that because of the court settlement between Union Carbide and the Indian government in 1989, it has no responsibility for the plant at Bhopal, which Union Carbide sold before the merger. "In the eyes of the highest courts of India, the Bhopal case is closed," said Dow President Michael Parker in 2001. Bhopal victims' groups disagree. They say more needs to be done to clean up the plant and compensate the survivors. They believe that Dow inherited these obligations when it bought Union Carbide.

A Bhopal in the United States?
Four months before the disaster in Bhopal, a smaller gas leak in the United States brought the dangers of hazardous chemicals close to home. On August 11, 1984, Union Carbide's pesticide plant in Institute, West Virginia, released 4,000 pounds (1,800 kilograms) of methylene chloride and aldicarb oxide. The toxic cloud spread over four nearby neighboring communities and caused the hospitalization of 135 people. The plant was similar in design to the Union Carbide plant in Bhopal. Investigators found that pressure gauges at the plant were broken, the alarms had been shut off, and the refrigeration units were not working.

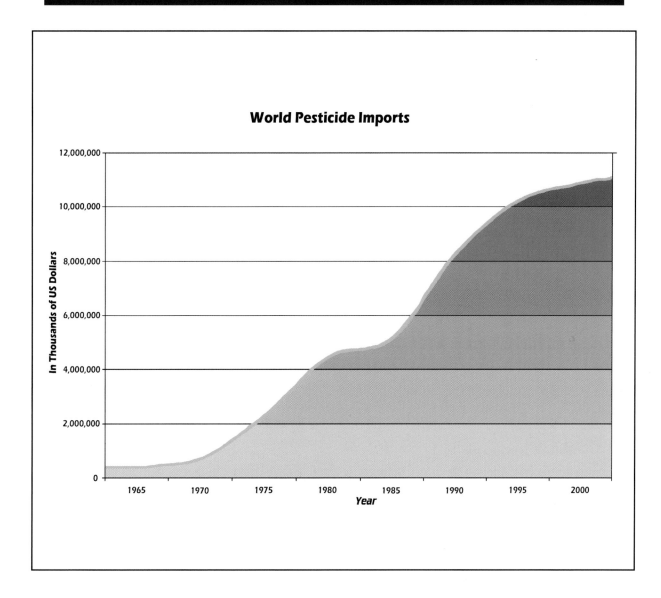

Union Carbide left hundreds of tons of toxic waste on the site of its Bhopal plant. Until mid-2001, the factory grounds were inaccessible without special permission from the government. Now the perimeter walls are broken and local children play in an area that remains dangerously contaminated.

by women who were exposed to the UCIL gas spill as children are more common in Bhopal than in other parts of India. And those children that live often suffer from birth defects that may have been caused by the chemicals in their mother's bodies or breast milk.

Many in Bhopal have long claimed that the abandoned Union Carbide plant is still leaking toxicants into the soil. In 2002, the Bhopal Municipal Corporation reported that the water near the factory is not safe to drink. It said some 20,000 people were at risk of health effects from the contaminated water. That same year, Dow Chemical, which had purchased Union Carbide in 2001, was forced by a U.S. court to release Union Carbide documents showing that the company knew the factory grounds were contaminated by hazardous chemicals.

Bhopal's residents are just as angry at the Indian government as they are

"The Death Toll Is Rising Every Day"

One group that has been active in trying to hold Dow Chemical responsible for cleanup at the Bhopal plant is Greenpeace, an environmental organization. Greenpeace has conducted site surveys at the Bhopal plant, looking for toxic materials they say have been dumped there. They have also staged protests by delivering barrels of contaminated soil and water to Dow offices in Europe and the United States.

"Today, the death toll stands at 20,000 and is rising every day," Greenpeace said in a 2002 press release on Bhopal. "Children born to survivors are suffering health problems and 150,000 people are in urgent need of medical attention."

Greenpeace activists delivered eighteen barrels of Bhopal's poisonous wastes to Dow's European headquarters in Horgen, Switzerland.

at Dow Chemical. They say their government did not acted swiftly enough to bring Warren Anderson to justice or to force Dow to clean up the factory site. Residents also claim that the government has done a poor job of distributing compensation, health care, and other aid to victims. The lives of the poor in Bhopal's slums have gotten worse because of the disaster, the victims say, and they demand that the Indian government do more about it.

As the legacy of the Bhopal gas tragedy enters its third decade, the streets of the ancient city are still the scene of angry protests. The memory of that horrible night lives on in the survivors, and it is being passed on to their children.

For those who lived through that night of death, grief has turned to rage. Whether that rage will ever lead to justice, no one can say.

Activists shout slogans during a torch-lit procession in Bhopal.

Time Line

1969	Union Carbide builds its first pesticide plant in Bhopal Union Carbide India Limited (UCIL) will run it.
1979	UCIL is expanded to allow production of MIC gas.
1982	A Union Carbide safety audit finds a high risk of toxic releases at the Bhopal plant and recommends changes.
1983	Safety systems at the Bhopal plant are shut down to save money.
1984	December 2: MIC workers begin flushing the pipes leading from the MIC tanks.
	December 3: A runaway reaction releases a cloud of MIC and other gases, killing thousands of people.
	December 18: The Indian government and UCIL complete Operation Faith, removing the last of the MIC gas from the Bhopal plant.
	December: Union Carbide Chairman Warren Anderson is arrested in Bhopal and told to leave the country.
1986	U.S. Congress passes the Emergency Planning and Community Right-to-Know Act in response to Bhopal.
1989	February: Indian Supreme Court orders Union Carbide to pay $470 million in damages.
1994	November: Union Carbide sells its interest in Union Carbide India Limited.
2001	February: Dow Chemical Company buys Union Carbide, becoming the world's largest chemical manufacturer.
2002	August: An Indian judge rejects the Indian government's attempts to reduce the criminal charges against Warren Anderson and orders his extradition to India for trial.

Glossary

autopsy the examination of a dead body to discover why the person or animal died; also called necropsy or postmortem.

carbaryl a very strong pesticide sold as the brand name Sevin® by UCIL.

chemical pneumonia a disease in which the lungs fill up with fluid as a result of inhaling toxic gas.

culpable homicide the crime of knowing that your actions helped cause a person's death without your direct involvement in the moment of death.

dichlorodiphenyltrichloroethane (DDT) a pesticide commonly used before 1970.

EPA (Environmental Protection Agency) the U.S. agency in charge of setting and enforcing quality standards and guidelines for the protection of the environment. The EPA was established in 1970.

environmentalist a person who works to protect air, water, and other natural resources from pollution or destruction.

fungicide a chemical that kills a fungus.

Green Revolution a movement during the 1960s and 1970s that aimed to boost food production in poor countries through the use of pesticides, fertilizers, and new farming methods.

Hindu a religion that believes in being reborn after death to better or worse lives, depending one's behavior.

homicide another name for murder.

hydrocyanic acid (high droh sigh AN ik) a very poisonous acid formed when MIC breaks down upon contact with water.

Madhya Pradesh (MAHD yah prah DESH) the large state in the middle of India where the city of Bhopal is located.

methyl isocyanate (MIC) (MEH thal eye so SIGH an eight) a poisonous compound used in the production of pesticides.

monomethylamine (mahn oh meh THAL ah meen) a toxic gas that forms when MIC reacts with water, iron, and other contaminants.

Muslim a follower of Islam, a religion that teaches submission to the will of Allah.

negligence (NEH glih jenz) not using proper caution.

pesticide any chemical that kills pests, such as insects.

phosgene (FOSS jeen) a highly toxic, irritating gas that can burn or corrode many substances.

Sevin® (SEH vihn) brand name for a carbaryl-based insecticide made by Union Carbide and Union Carbide India Limited.

Sikh (SEEK) a follower of Sikhism, a religion that teaches devotion to and remembrance of God at all times; it combines elements of Hinduism and Islam.

Temik® a very strong fungicide.

toxic a poison; also, the effects of a poison.

toxicant any poisonous substance, sometimes created by humans.

toxin a poison that has biological origins; can cause the production of antibodies in the blood of humans or animals and/or changes in that creature's DNA.

For More Information

Books

Bhopal. Great Disasters, Reforms, and Ramifications (series).
   John Riddle (Chelsea House)

Cartoon Guide to the Environment. Larry Gonick (HarperCollins)

Chemical Accident. Christopher Lampton (Millbrook Press)

*Five Past Midnight in Bhopal: The Epic Story of the World's
   Deadliest Industrial Disaster.* Dominique LaPierre (Warner)

One Good Apple: Growing Our Food for the Sake of the Earth.
   Catherine Paladino (Houghton Mifflin)

Videos

Emerging Powers: India — An Insider's Guide. (Wall Street Journal Video)

Modern Marvels: Farming Technology. (A & E Home Video)

Web Sites

Bhopal.Net: News, Information, Action
www.bhopal.net

The Bhopal Medical Appeal
www.bhopal.org

Dow Chemical Global Public Report
www.dow.com/publicreport/2001/worldclass/bhopal.htm

Greenpeace: Bhopal
www.greenpeaceusa.org/bhopal

Union Carbide, Bhopal: Incident Review
www.bhopal.com/review.htm

Index

Index (continued)